5/08

AWESOME ATHLETES

BRETT FAVRE

Jill C. Wheeler
ABDO & Daughters

visit us at
www.abdopub.com

Published by Abdo & Daughters, 4940 Viking Drive, Suite 622, Edina, Minnesota 55435.
Copyright © 1998 by Abdo Consulting Group, Inc., Pentagon Tower, P.O. Box 36036, Minneapolis, Minnesota 55435 USA. International copyrights reserved in all countries. No part of this book may be reproduced in any form without written permission from the publisher.

Printed in the United States.

Cover and Interior Photo credits: Duomo
Allsports

Edited by Kal Gronvall

Library of Congress Cataloging-in-Publication Data

Wheeler, Jill C., 1964-
    Brett Favre /Jill C. Wheeler.
    p. cm. -- (Awesome athletes)
    Includes index.
    Summary: A biography which discusses the personal life and Football career of the quarter back who led the Green Bay Packers to victory in Super Bowl XXXI
    ISBN 1-56239-844-X
    1. Favre, Brett--Juvenile literature. 2. Football players--United States--Biography-- Juvenile literature. 3. Green Bay packers (Football team)--Juvenile literature [1. Favre, Brett. 2. Football players. I. Title. II. Series.
    GV939.F29W54   1998   97-26587
    796.332'092--dc21   CIP
    [B]   AC

Contents

Young Superstar

The 1996-97 **National Football League (NFL)** season had many fans concerned. It seemed like there weren't many good quarterbacks in the league. So many of the quarterbacks were just too young.

As the playoffs neared, the top-ranking quarterback in the game was only 27 years old. He wore the Number 4 jersey for the Green Bay Packers.

This young athlete had been in the NFL for just five years. In that time, however, he had tallied 1,667 completions on 2,691 attempts, 18,720 total yards, and 147 touchdowns. In the 1996 regular season alone, he completed 325 of 543 for 3,899 yards and had 39 touchdowns.

Most importantly, he took the Packers all the way to a **Super Bowl** victory over the New England Patriots. It was the team's first in 29 years.

The Pack was back. And no one was more thrilled than the team's starting quarterback, Brett Favre.

Brett Favre celebrating after a touchdown at Tampa Stadium

A Natural Athlete

Brett Lorenzo Favre (pronounced "farv") was born October 10, 1969, in Gulfport, Mississippi. He grew up in Kiln, Mississippi, the second of four children born to Irvin and Bonita Favre. Irvin was the football coach at local Hancock North Central High School. Bonita was a special education teacher at the same school.

Brett, along with his brothers Scott and Jeff, took turns as quarterback for the high school football team. All were gifted athletes with a passion for sports. Brett earned five **letters** in baseball and three in football. "Of the three, Brett was the most talented," Irvin remembers. "He was rawboned, brute strength, plus he was smart."

"Brett was quiet, the most reserved of the bunch," Bonita recalls. He also was stubborn, refusing to use anyone else's cup or share a bedroom with his brothers. Also, he didn't seem to mind pain. "If you slapped him

Favre at the 1997 Super Bowl in New Orleans, Louisiana.

when he was little, he'd say it didn't hurt," she added. "He would never give in."

Even as a child, Brett dreamed of being a football player. He did push-ups every night before bed. He ran the half-mile from his house to the road every day as well. More than anything, he wanted to play for the Dallas Cowboys.

When he was in ninth grade he met another Cowboys fan named Deanna Tynes. Like Brett, she was a talented athlete. "Don't throw it so hard," his father once scolded him when Brett and Deanna were playing catch. "Why?" Brett asked. "She's catching them."

Brett and Deanna dated through high school. In the fall of 1987, Deanna followed Brett to the University of Southern Mississippi. Today she is his wife and the mother of their seven-year-old daughter, Brittany.

Brett resting on the bench.

8

Brett with wife Deanna and daughter Brittany.

Storming
Southern Miss'

Brett enrolled at the University of Southern Mississippi in Hattiesburg, Mississippi, in 1987. He received the school's last football scholarship by chance. The player who was supposed to have it never attended the school. At the beginning of his freshman year, he was number seven to start as quarterback. He moved up quickly. By the third game that year he was starting for the university's Golden Eagles.

Tragedy struck, however, the July before his senior season. Brett was on his way home from a fishing trip. He hit a patch of loose gravel and lost control of his car. The car flipped in the air three times and hit a tree. His brother, Scott, had been following him. Scott had to smash the car's windshield with a golf club to pull Brett out of the car.

The accident left him with a severe **concussion**, fractured **vertebra**, and many cuts and bruises. Doctors had to remove 30 inches of his large intestine. He remembers lying in his hospital bed listening to the TV. The announcer was saying, "Will Brett Favre ever play football again?" He vowed to himself that he would.

Brett Favre playing for the University of Southern Mississippi.

"Every day I tried to do a little more," he said. "Whirlpool, ice, lifting weights. Gradually, I fought my way back."

Thousands of fans applauded wildly when Brett ran on to Legion Field in Birmingham, Alabama, on September 8. He was 35 pounds lighter and his uniform sagged around him. Yet even the fans who had come to cheer for Alabama cheered for Brett. Their cheers quickly faded, however, as Brett led Southern Mississippi to a surprise win over Alabama.

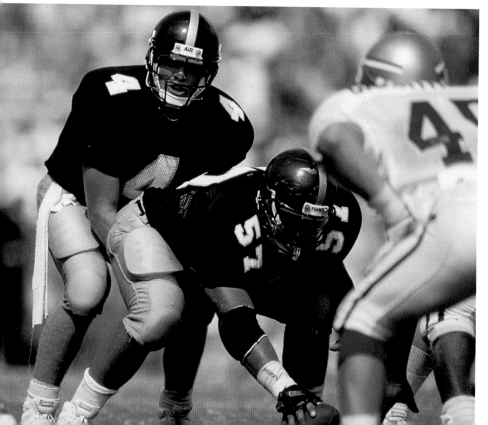

Favre over center for Southern Mississippi.

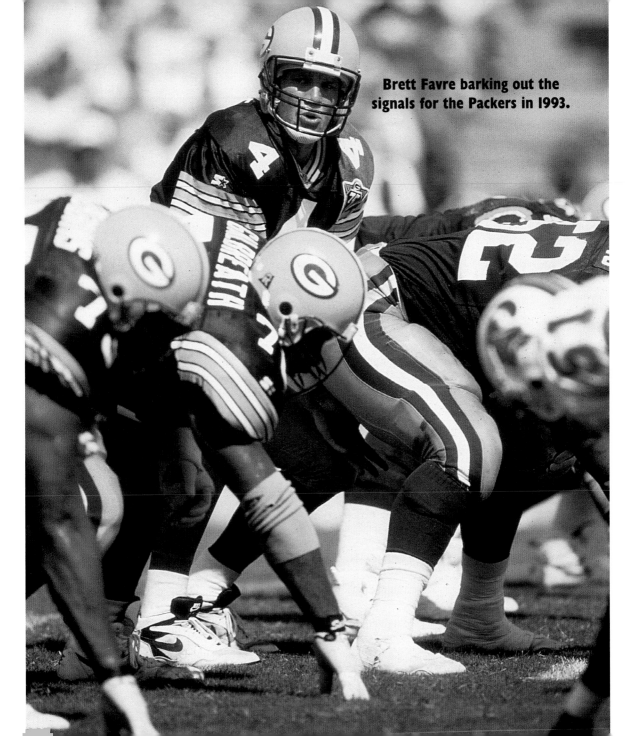

Brett Favre barking out the signals for the Packers in 1993.

THE MAKING OF AN AWESOME ATHLETE

Brett Favre could be one of the NFL's best quarterbacks ever.

1969	1987	1991	1992
Born October 10, in Gulfport, MS.	Began playing for the University of Southern Mississippi.	Drafted by Atlanta Falcons and spent most of his time on the bench.	Traded to Green Bay Packers and was starting quarterback by the third game.

How Awesome Is He?

Favre's performance in 1994 was worthy of a Pro Bowl bid, but he wasn't selected for the team. Compare his stats to those of the quarterbacks who were chosen.

	Att.	Comp.	Yards
Troy Aikman	361	233	2,676
Brett Favre	**582**	**363**	**3,882**
Warren Moon	601	371	4,264
Steve Young	461	324	3,969

BRETT FAVRE

AGE: 28
HEIGHT: 6 feet 2 inches
WEIGHT: 225 pounds
TEAM: Green Bay Packers

1993

Became one of only seven NFL quarterbacks to start all 16 games. First in NFC with 318 completions. Made first **Pro Bowl** appearance.

1994

Second to Steve Young in MVP ballot. Threw 23 touchdowns over last eight games of the season.

1995

Selected NFL MVP. Earns 86.8 career quarterback rating — fourth highest in league history.

1997

Won Superbowl XXXI in New Orleans, Louisiana against New England Patriots.

- Only second player to receive NFL's MVP Award two years in a row (1995 & 1996).
- Third fastest quarterback to throw 100 NFL touchdown passes.
- Number four passer in NFL history with a rating of 86.8.
- First quarterback ever to throw more than 30 touchdown passes in each of three consecutive seasons (1994-96).

Highlights

On to the NFL

Brett led Southern Mississippi to two bowl victories in his college career. He set six school passing **records**. Off the field, he had a reputation as someone who would stay out at parties all night and play a game the next day.

He continued his wild streak even after he was chosen as a second-round **draft** pick by the Atlanta Falcons in 1991. Unfortunately, he spent most of the season for the Falcons on the sidelines. By the end of the season he had thrown just five passes and completed none of them.

The Packers traded a first-round draft pick to get Brett in 1992, and that angered many Green Bay Packer fans. Brett didn't think he would play for the Packers, either, because they already had a talented starting quarterback. His name was Don Majkowski.

Brett's opportunity to play came in the third game of the 1992 season against the Cincinnati Bengals. The

Packers were down by 17 points when Majkowski was injured. Brett stepped in and led them to a one-point victory over the Bengals. He's been the starting quarterback for the Packers ever since.

Brett sitting on the bench at Lambeau Field.

Life of a Quarterback

Being a quarterback is tougher than most people think. "My first couple of years in Green Bay I realized I was doing the hardest thing in sports," Brett said. "We had 16 quarterback meetings a week. Learning our offense—any pro offense, really—is harder than learning chemistry or calculus."

Green Bay uses a complicated play structure called the West Coast Offense. The quarterback is the brain of that offense. He must read the situation on the field and make split-second decisions. It took a long time for Brett to learn his job. That frustrated him.

"In the first year or so I don't think anybody on our team knew exactly what we were doing," he said. "I struggled and I struggled for a long time. But think about it: I got thrown into the toughest offense in the game as a starter at 22. Every other guy who's played it sat for a year or two and learned."

Brett rapidly improved. By 1995, Brett topped the NFL with 359 completions for 4,413 yards and 38 touchdowns. The Packers finished the regular season 11-5 and headed for the playoffs. The Pack beat the Falcons and the San Francisco 49ers, only to lose to Brett's old favorite, the Dallas Cowboys. Despite the loss, Brett was named the NFL's **Most Valuable Player (MVP)** for 1995.

Yet his success has come at a price—injuries. Brett suffered a bruised hip in 1991. He separated his shoulder in 1992. The following year, he badly bruised his thigh. In 1995, he was diagnosed with a **hernia**. Like so many other football players, he relied on pain pills to help him make it through the games.

Beating an Addiction

Brett was in the hospital again on February 27, 1996. He was recovering from ankle surgery. Suddenly, his body began jerking around in **convulsions**. His daughter, Brittany, asked Deanna, "Mom, is he going to die?"

Brett didn't die, but he did realize something important. He was addicted to a painkiller called Vicodin. Being a football player is hard on the body. Football players often are injured and routinely roughed-up during their games. Brett was no exception. He began taking Vicodin to deal with his injuries. Eventually, his body became addicted to it. It made him feel better even when he wasn't in pain.

Brett thought that the drug helped him to manage stress. "The pills enabled me to escape the realities of being a quarterback and a star," he said. He began to pop the pills all the time. He would take the drug and then stay up all night studying his playbook or watching TV. People around him began to notice a change. "He was really different at

Charles Haley roughs up Favre.

night," said Deanna. "He wasn't himself. He was defensive all the time." Deanna asked him to get help.

Brett finally did seek help after doctors said that his addiction might have caused the **seizure**. He entered a drug rehabilitation center. He said it was as hard as **boot camp**. Yet afterwards, he was glad he had gone and kicked his addiction.

"It was hard," he said. "I was someone used to doing what I wanted to do. But now I feel I have ways to handle stress without pills. The bigger thing I've learned is to turn to the people around me. . . . Before, I was keeping a lot of things inside me."

The Packers are defeated at Dallas Stadium in 1996.

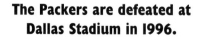

Brett Favre relaxing during the off season.

Charging to the Top

Brett began the 1996 season a changed player. He no longer took pain pills. He didn't drink alcohol. He was committed to being the best quarterback in the NFL. He was committed to beating the Dallas Cowboys. And he was committed to taking the Green Bay Packers all the way to the **Super Bowl**.

In their first game of the regular season, Brett threw four touchdown passes. The Packers beat rival Tampa Bay Buccaneers 34-3. It was the largest margin of victory in an opener since the 1965 Packers crushed Pittsburgh 41-9.

The Packers kept racking up wins as Favre racked up points. He hit an awesome 24 of 35 passes for 281 yards against the Detroit Lions. "You see why [Favre] was MVP," said one of the Detroit coaches after the game. "He is such a great, great player."

At the end of the regular season, Green Bay had won all but three games. They clinched the division title with a 35-14 win over the San Francisco 49ers. Next they won the National Football Conference (NFC) championship with a 30-13 win over the league's new North Carolina Panthers.

Brett was just one game away from his dream: a **Super Bowl** victory. And he would be playing the biggest game of his life just one hour from the Mississippi **bayous** where he spent his childhood.

The Packers celebrate another victory, thanks to Brett.

25

Super Bowl XXXI

It was January 26, 1997. Screaming fans packed the Louisiana Superdome in New Orleans, Louisiana, to see **Super Bowl** XXXI. Football fans around the world were watching to see the showdown between the two young quarterbacks.

Twenty-four-year-old Drew Bledsoe felt the pressure. As quarterback for American Football Conference (AFC) Champion New England Patriots, he had a challenge ahead of him. No AFC team had won a Super Bowl in more than 12 years.

Meanwhile, 27-year-old Brett Favre was hoping to bring home a win for Green Bay. It had been more than 20 years since Green Bay fans had celebrated a Super Bowl win.

Brett showed his stuff just 3:32 minutes into the game. He threw a 54-yard touchdown pass to Andre Risen. It was his first pass attempt of the game, and it put the Packers on top 7-0.

He went on to set a new **Super Bowl record** for the longest touchdown pass. Fifty-six seconds into the second quarter, he threw an 81 yard strike to Antonio Freeman for a touchdown. It put the Packers back on top 17-14. In the third quarter, with just 1:11 minutes remaining, he capped a nine-play, 74-yard drive with a two-yard touchdown run. The Packer's lead grew to 27-14.

When the clock ran out on Super Bowl XXXI, Green Bay had won. Brett could add another dream to his list of wishes come true.

Brett Favre faces the media circus at the 1997 Super Bowl.

Giving Something Back

Brett has come a long way from being the quarterback for Hancock North Central High School. "Nobody knows how hard it is to get to the top and how hard it is to stay on top," Brett says. "Now that I'm here, it doesn't make it any easier."

Brett still enjoys having fun with his family and friends. He also realizes it's important to give something back to the people who have supported his football career. He began the Favre Fourward Foundation to help do that.

The foundation raises money to give to charities. Each year he holds a charity golf outing. In 1997, he raised more than $150,000. Sometimes he holds autograph signing sessions and donates a portion of those funds to charity, too.

Brett, Deanna, and Brittany now live in Green Bay. Though millions of people watch him on TV, he tries to lead a normal life. He still does push-ups every night, just like when he was young. Except now Brittany gets to sit on his back while he does them.

Only time will tell which new **records** he will set. Yet one thing is for sure. Brett has proven to be an Awesome Athlete.

Favre looking for the open receiver.

GLOSSARY

Bayou - A slow moving body of water like a marsh.

Boot camp - The place where new soldiers go for very hard training.

Concussion - An injury caused by a blow to the head.

Convulsion - A sudden contraction of the body's muscles.

Draft - An event held in April where NFL teams choose college players. The worst team gets the first pick.

Hernia - A type of injury.

Letter - An award given to a high school athlete.

Most Valuable Player (MVP) - An award given to the best player in the league or Super Bowl.

National Football League (NFL) - A professional football league in the United States consisting of a National and American Conference, each with 15 teams.

Pro Bowl - An All-Star game played at the end of the season in Hawaii. The best players at their position get to play.

Record - The best that has ever been done in a certain event.

Seizure - A sudden attack.

Super Bowl - The NFL championship game played between the American and National conference champions.

Vertebra - One of the parts of the backbone.

PASS IT ON

Tell Others Something Special About Your Favorite Sports or Athletes

What makes your favorite athlete awesome? Do you think you have a chance to be an Awesome Athlete? Tell us about your favorite plays, tournaments, and anything else that has to do with sports. We want to hear from you!

To get posted on ABDO & Daughters website E-mail us at "sports@abdopub.com"

Index